PRAYER
FOR A CHILD

BY RACHEL FIELD
PICTURES BY ELIZABETH ORTON JONES

Aladdin Books

Macmillan Publishing Company
New York

Collier Macmillan Publishers
London

Aladdin Books
Macmillan Publishing Company
866 Third Avenue, New York, N.Y. 10022
Collier Macmillan Canada, Inc.

Library of Congress catalog card number: 84-70991

Prayer for a Child is also published in a
hardcover edition by Macmillan Publishing Company
First Collier Books Edition 1973
First Collier Books Trade Paperback Edition 1984

ISBN 0-02-043070-1

Printed in the United States of America

10 9 8 7 6

FOR HANNAH

PRAYER FOR A CHILD

Bless this milk and bless this bread.
Bless this soft and waiting bed
Where I presently shall be
Wrapped in sweet security.
Through the darkness, through the night
Let no danger come to fright
My sleep till morning once again
Beckons at the window pane.
Bless the toys whose shapes I know,
The shoes that take me to and fro
Up and down and everywhere.
Bless my little painted chair.
Bless the lamplight, bless the fire,
Bless the hands that never tire
In their loving care of me.
Bless my friends and family.
Bless my Father and my Mother
And keep us close to one another.
Bless other children, far and near,
And keep them safe and free from fear.
So let me sleep and let me wake
In peace and health, for Jesus' sake.

                              Amen.

less this milk and bless this bread.

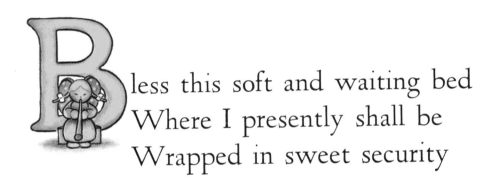

Bless this soft and waiting bed
Where I presently shall be
Wrapped in sweet security

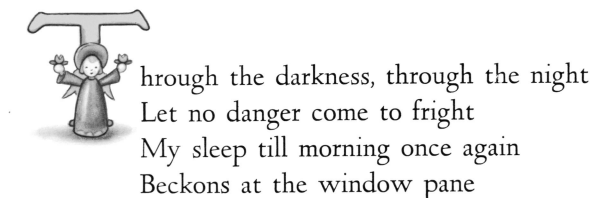

hrough the darkness, through the night
Let no danger come to fright
My sleep till morning once again
Beckons at the window pane

less the toys whose shapes I know

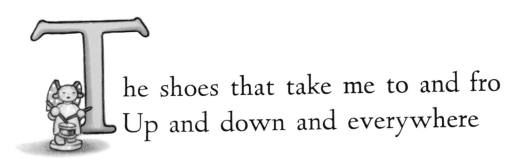

The shoes that take me to and fro
Up and down and everywhere

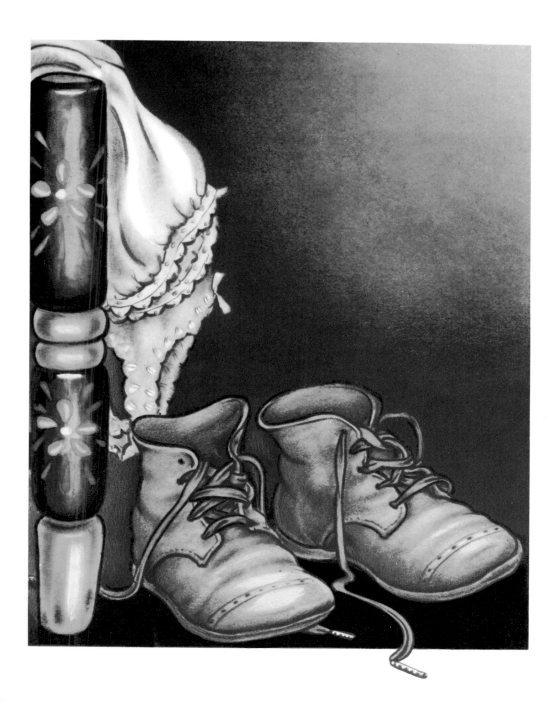

less my little painted chair

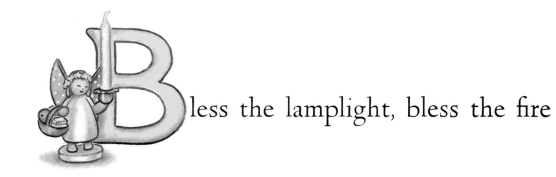 less the lamplight, bless the fire

less the hands that never tire
In their loving care of me

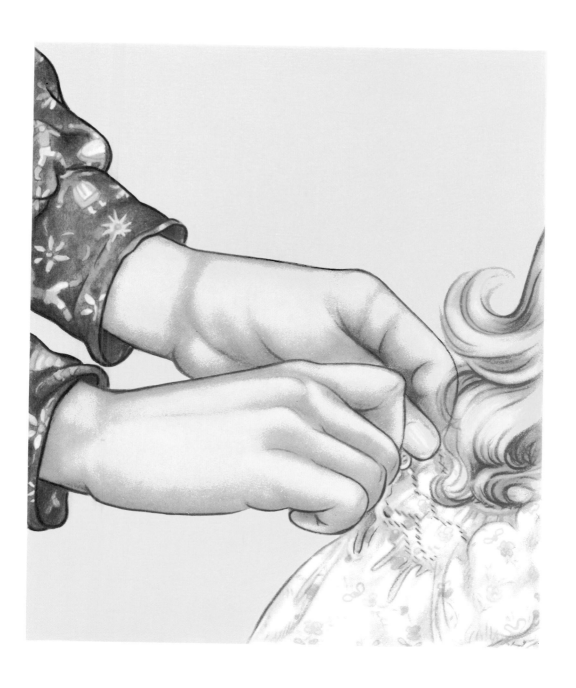

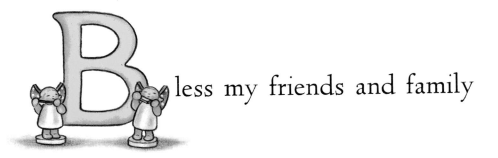less my friends and family

less my Father and my Mother
And keep us close to one another

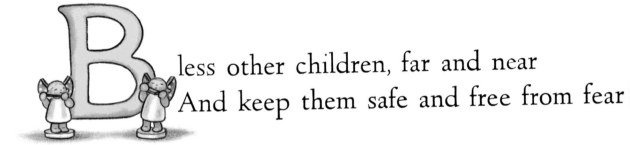

less other children, far and near
And keep them safe and free from fear

So let me sleep and let me wake
In peace and health, for Jesus' sake

men